Sports Stars

MARY LOU RETTON

Gold Medal Gymnast

By Hal Lundgren

CHILDRENS PRESS ™

CHICAGO

Cover photograph: © Diane Johnson
Inside photographs courtesy of the following:
© Diane Johnson, pages 6, 9, 17, 23, 24, 26, 31, 37,
40, and 43
© Michael Miller 1984, pages 10, 13, 15, 19, 21, 34,
and 39
Ira Golden, pages 29 and 33

Library of Congress Cataloging in Publication Data

Lundgren, Hal.
    Mary Lou Retton, gold medal gymnast.

    (Sport stars)
    Summary: Recounts the professional life of sixteen-year-old
Mary Lou Retton, who won five medals in the 1984 Olympics.
    1. Retton, Mary Lou, 1968-   —Juvenile literature.
2. Gymnasts—United States—Biography—Juvenile literature.
3. Olympic Games (23rd: 1984: Los Angeles, Calif.)—
Juvenile literature. [1. Retton, Mary Lou, 1968-
2. Gymnasts] I. Title. II. Series.
GV460.2.R47L86 1985   796.4'1'0924 [B] [92] 84-29313
ISBN 0-516-04346-3

1 2 3 4 5 6 7 8 9 10 R 94 93 92 91 90 89 88 87 86 85

Sports Stars

MARY LOU RETTON

Gold Medal Gymnast

"Dynamite."

That's what a photographer said when he saw Mary Lou Retton.

"She's dynamite," he said a second time. "What a smile! I've taken many pictures. But I've never seen such a bright smile."

That's Mary Lou. Dynamite. At 4 feet, 10 inches tall and only 95 pounds, she's "little dynamite." She is as famous for her personality as she is for her gymnastics. And she is the most famous gymnast ever.

Most Americans did not know much about Mary Lou Retton before the 1984 Olympics. But she was famous in Fairmont, West Virginia, where she grew up. Her parents still live there.

Mary Lou also was famous in Houston, Texas. She moved there to train with gymnastics coach Bela Karolyi. Before Karolyi moved to the United States from Romania in 1981, he coached Romania's Olympic gymnastics team. His most famous student was Nadia Comaneci. She was the Olympic champion in 1976.

People who lived outside Fairmont and Houston knew little about Mary Lou. She won the America's Cup in the spring of 1984. But only people who follow gymnastics knew how much that meant.

Before the 1984 Olympics in Los Angeles, not many people knew about Mary Lou, the gymnast.

Now millions of people know about Mary Lou and her charming smile.

It wasn't until Mary Lou won at the 1984 Olympics that everybody knew about her. If someone in her teens could ever be a star overnight, it was Mary Lou.

You know about her smile. She also is great in the four gymnastics events for women. They are: the uneven parallel bars, balance beam, floor exercise, and the vault. She also makes people who watch her feel good about themselves.

Mary Lou comes from a sports family. Her father, Ron, played basketball at the University of West Virginia. His team almost won the national championship in 1959. He was not tall, either—only 5 feet, 7 inches.

Mary Lou is the youngest of the five Retton children. Her three older brothers and an older sister played sports. They played baseball, basketball, and gymnastics. Her sister was an All-American in gymnastics. But no American girl had ever won an individual medal at the Olympics.

Mary Lou was born in Fairmont on January 24, 1968. She was always a great talent. She is stronger than most of her opponents. Her strength makes her the world's No. 1 vaulter. But she couldn't be an Olympic champion with just talent. The man who might be the best gymnastics coach in the world taught her.

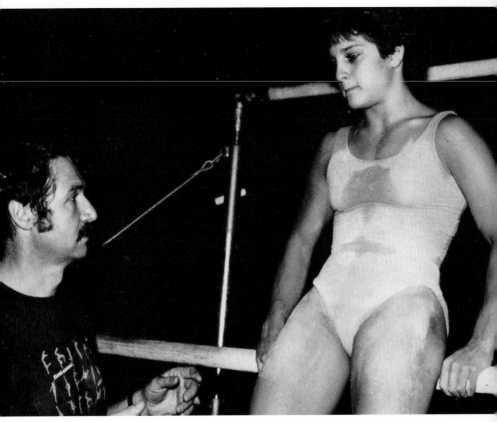

Beli Karolyi, Mary Lou's coach, talks to her about working on the uneven parallel bars.

Karolyi's country, Romania, is small. Romania is a Communist country. The people are not free. They do not have fair elections. There is no free press. People cannot speak against the government.

Bela Karolyi and his wife loved Romania. It was their home. But they were tired of their country's unfair laws. When they came to the United States for a visit in 1981, they stayed. They looked around the United States for a place to teach gymnastics. Their gymnastics school in Romania was the best in the world.

Bela Karolyi picked Houston as his new home. He did not have much money. He opened his school in an old, metal building. It was not fancy. Because his school in Romania was so good, gymnasts from all over the U.S. came to Houston. They wanted to be in Karolyi's new school.

"We have the most powerful team in the country," Karolyi said proudly.

Mary Lou Retton was one of the girls who decided to come to Houston. She had heard of Karolyi years ago. She wanted to join his school. Then, near the end of 1982, she was in a meet against his team.

"I wanted to be a part of it," she said.

She moved to Houston right away.

Soon, Mary Lou and Diane Durham, who moved to Houston from Gary, Indiana, were the best gymnasts on the Karolyi team.

Life was not easy for Mary Lou. She had to leave her family in West Virginia. She lived with a Houston family. They had a daughter in the Karolyi school.

"Sometimes," she said, "I got homesick."

Mary Lou could not go to school as do most teenagers. She was busy with gymnastics. There wasn't enough time. She took correspondence courses. It was like doing homework all the time and never going to class.

There was little time for dating and parties. Other sports were pushed out of her life, too. Gymnastics was the center of her life. She was pleased to hear the things Karolyi said about her.

"Mary Lou is the strongest," he said. "She has the most potential of anyone. There is no physical comparison with Nadia Comaneci. Mary Lou's strength is so unusual for a girl."

For a while, it all seemed easy. Mary Lou practiced for hundreds of hours. She won major events. She kept winning. In the spring of 1984, the Los Angeles Olympics looked like just another meet she would win. Then it happened. She hurt a knee.

Mary Lou is strong and works well on the balance beam. Her coach, Karolyi, watches her work.

"My knee just locked up on me," she said sadly. "It was the worst feeling I've ever had."

All at once, the Olympics seemed so far away. Perhaps too far away for her to reach.

"I thought it was all over for me," Mary Lou said.

It wasn't all over for her.

Doctors have a new way of fixing some knee injuries.

Instead of a regular operation, they put a small tube into the knee. It does not hurt. The doctors are able to see through the tube to the inside of the knee. They can fix the knee through the tube. When the doctors are finished they put a Band-Aid on the knee. Then the person can go home right away.

In the Olympics, Mary Lou received a bronze medal for her floor exercises.

One week after knee surgery, Mary Lou was back practicing gymnastics.

This new way of fixing knees has a long name. It is called arthroscopy (AR-thros-co-py).

Mary Lou had arthroscopy June 15, 1984. She was walking well the next day. One week later, she was working out.

"It's a miracle to me," she said. "I don't have any pain at all. It was tight for a couple of days. But I worked out on a bicycle and went swimming. That helped a lot. My doctor can't believe how quickly I recovered."

Neither could Bela Karolyi.

"It's like the eighth wonder of the world to me," he said. "It's amazing.

Mary Lou says Karolyi is a tough coach, but she likes that.

"She had a very bad injury. Twelve days later, you didn't know anything had happened. I give her a lot of credit. She is very determined."

Karolyi also said, "I think Mary Lou can win three medals."

A regular operation would have kept Mary Lou out of the Olympics. She would not have practiced for six or eight weeks after the operation. Eight weeks after the operation, the Olympics would have been over. Mary Lou could not have won.

Mary Lou got well so quickly that her knee was not a problem. Nothing else got in her way, either. She was too determined to let that happen.

Many TV, radio, newspaper, and magazine people came to see Mary Lou. They all wanted to talk to her.

"It was hectic," she said. "I was prepared for it. A lot of people told me it would be like this."

Karolyi wanted the news people to talk and write about gymnastics. But there wasn't time to talk to all of them. Karolyi was coaching Mary Lou and Diane Durham. Then another star came to his school. She was Julianne McNamara. She was born in New York and raised in California. Nearly three years older than Mary Lou, Julianne was an Olympic veteran. She was considered America's No. 1 female gymnast on the uneven parallel bars.

Mary Lou sits with Julianne McNamara during the Olympics.

"Mary Lou Retton and Julianne McNamara are going to be pioneers," Karolyi once said. "We are building champions in our school. The future looks very good."

Mary Lou's future was the brightest. She could sense it. She even spoke about it.

"I think I have a strong chance to win the gold medal in the vault. I also have a good chance in the floor exercise."

"She's the best vaulter in the world," Karolyi said. "She has dominated U.S. gymnastics since 1983. I knew she had the physical ability. Her mental outlook is what has made her improve so fast. She has a very open and pleasant personality. She also has a very strong desire to win."

Julianne, Mary Lou, and their teammates celebrate during the Olympics.

As the photographer said, Mary Lou was dynamite.

Before the Olympics, she won the International Gymnastics Cup in Los Angeles. She won the American Cup in New York twice. She became the first American to win the Chunichi Cup in Japan.

She also came up with a special flip. She would swing from the high bar in the uneven parallel bars. She would hit the lower bar. She would flip to a sitting position on the high bar.

It was called the Retton Flip.

Bela Karolyi workouts made her get better. But she could not have improved if workouts had been easy.

Since she was seven years old, Mary Lou has been in gymnastics.

Although practicing is hard work, Mary Lou can still smile.

"It was a shock when I first came to him," Mary Lou said. "His workouts were hard. I wasn't used to them. He's a tough coach. But that's what I like."

She had practiced hard. She had the Retton Flip. It was time for Los Angeles and the Olympics. She was ready.

Was she ever ready!

Mary Lou won five medals. One gold. Two silver. Two bronze.

Even at 4 feet, 10 inches, it would be hard to call her "little dynamite" anymore.

From the first moment, Mary Lou was great. In the first round of team gymnastics, she won the vault and floor exercises. She placed third in floor exercise and uneven parallel bars. She was more than just a heroine in America. World-wide television made her a heroine in most countries.

Karolyi's home country, Romania, won the team event. Mary Lou and her U.S. teammates were second. Russia, another strong team, did not come to the Olympics. Even with Russia in the Olympics, Karolyi said America would have been in second place.

Mary Lou was pleased with her start. She said, "I was nearly flawless. I was happy with the way things went."

The most important part of the Olympics was yet to come. It was the all-around championship. Mary Lou went out and won it. At 16, she was an American princess—and an American sweetheart.

She had also changed gymnastics.

Olga Korbut was the champion in 1972. Nadia Comaneci, Karolyi's student, won in 1976. They were both slender. You could have called them butterflies.

Mary Lou is built more like a speed skater than a dancer. She has more muscles than Korbut and Comaneci, the "butterflies."

"The time of the butterfly is over," Karolyi said. "There will be no more butterflies."

Being a good gymnast is difficult, but Mary Lou makes it look so easy.

In the 1984 Olympic games, the U.S. team won the silver medal.

Karolyi meant that there will be more strong girls in gymnastics, thanks to Mary Lou.

"It is girls like Mary Lou who will support a harder level of gymnastics," Karolyi said. "She is strong and quick. She is a powerful girl. There will be more like her. This is good. We are not teaching ballet. We are gymnasts."

Even if there are gymnasts as strong as Mary Lou, will they be as determined? Will they work as hard? Will they give it so much time?

In the end, Mary Lou's effort made her win.

"Mary Lou is a hardworking girl," Karolyi said. "In the two years before the Olympics, she never said, 'No, I can't do it.' She never said, 'I'm just too tired.' She never said, 'I'm having an off day.' She always had a good attitude."

Looking back at all her time and work, Mary Lou said everything was worth it.

"Everybody leaves home sometime," she said. "My parents were 100 percent behind me. You have to have the right coaching in gymnastics. If I hadn't gone to his school, there's no way I would have won. I came to win. I achieved it. It's all so great."

Mary Lou still loves gymnastics. Some of her teammates on the U.S. team have retired. She will go on training. She will go on smiling.

"Don't ever stop smiling," one fan told her after the Olympics.

"Don't worry," Mary Lou answered. "I never will."

The 1988 Olympics are a long way off. But Mary Lou says she wants to be in them. She will be 20 years old then. There might be some 16 year old ready to defeat her. Another dynamite gymnast.

Mary Lou still isn't sure if there will be time for boys.

"I haven't had time for them. Boys can wait. But not for long," she giggled.

CHRONOLOGY

1968—Mary Lou Retton is born to an athletic family in Fairmont, West Virginia, January 24.

1982—After competing against Bela Karolyi's team in December, she decides to move to Houston with her parents' permission and enroll in the Karolyi school.

1983—In December, less than one year after she started studying under Karolyi, Mary Lou becomes the first American woman to win Japan's Chunichi Cup.

1984—Now a dominant gymnast, Mary Lou wins her second straight American Cup in March.

—Mary Lou looks like a cinch gold-medalist in May when she wins the U.S. Championship.

—After persistent knee swelling, she has an operation June 15. It is successful. She is back in training one week later.

—The big day! August 3! Mary Lou wins the Olympic women's all-around gymnastics championship in Los Angeles.

—Within four days of the win, Mary Lou has had about 70 offers to do TV, magazine, and newspaper ads.

—The Olympic flame is put out August 12. Mary Lou leaves with five medals.

—On September 1, Mary Lou begins training for what she hopes will be a place on America's 1988 Olympic team.

ABOUT THE AUTHOR

Hal Lundgren is editor of *Texas Sportsworld*, a regional magazine that began publishing in 1984. He is a former pro football writer for the *Houston Chronicle* and public relations director for the San Francisco 49ers.

Mr Lundgren has served as a member of the Pro Football Hall of Fame selections committee, president of Houston Sportswriters and Sportscasters Association, and Houston board of directors of Big Brothers-Big Sisters. He is married and has two sons. He enjoys playing the trumpet, basketball, fishing, and classical music.

Mr Lundgren has written four books for Childrens Press: *Earl Campbell: The Texas Tornado, Calvin Murphy: The Giant Slayer, Moses Malone: Philadelphia's Peerless Center,* and *NFL Superstars.*